Past Papers
Question Bank AMC 10
vol. I

Comprehensive Collection of AMC10 Past Papers

AMC10 Past Paper Questions Categorized by Topic

Introduction

Welcome to the world of AMC10 problem-solving! In this book by Kay, we present a unique approach to help students excel in the AMC10 examination. The book's distinct features aim to enhance performance and guide students towards better results.

The first notable aspect is the organization. Problems from past AMC10 exams are categorized by content, allowing students to focus on specific topics and develop a deeper understanding. By providing a structured learning experience, students can strengthen their problem-solving skills.

Another crucial element is the careful determination of problem difficulty. Each problem is ranked according to its level of complexity, ensuring a diverse range of challenges. Similar problems closely aligned with the actual exam questions provide additional practice opportunities, familiarizing students with the exam format.

Comprehensive learning is ensured through detailed solutions. Step-by-step explanations accompany each problem, guiding students through the thought processes and strategies for arriving at correct answers. This empowers students to approach problems confidently and strengthen their abilities.

The book's purpose is to equip students with the necessary tools to achieve better results in the AMC10 examination. By providing curated problems, determining difficulty levels, and offering in-depth solutions, we aim to enhance performance and foster a passion for mathematics.

Embark on this journey of problem-solving, and let the challenges within these pages propel you towards success in the AMC10 examination!

Table of Contents

vol. II continued ...

3. Counting and Probability

4. Number Theory

5. Others

01. ▉▉☐☐☐

Assuming Albert cycled at a constant speed throughout, how many laps did he complete in the first 27 minutes if he cycled a total of 15 laps in 57 minutes?

(AMC 10A problem)

(A) 6

(B) 7

(C) 8

(D) 9

(E) 10

Solving Strategy

We can start by using a proportion to find the speed at which Albert cycled. Then, we can use this speed and the given time to find the number of laps he completed in the first 27 minutes.

02. ■□□□□

John can run 10 laps around a track in 30 minutes at a constant speed. How many laps did he run in the first 12 minutes?

(AMC 10A similar problem)

(A) 4

(B) 5

(C) 6

(D) 7

(E) 8

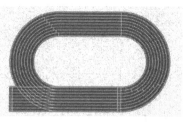

03. ■■□□□

Measuring automobile fuel efficiency can vary depending on the country, with some using miles per gallon while others measure in liters per 100 kilometers. Let A represent the number of miles equivalent to 1 kilometer, and let B represent the number of liters equivalent to 1 gallon.

Which of the following gives the fuel efficiency in liters per 100 kilometers for a car that gets C miles per gallon?

(AMC 10A problem)

(A) $\dfrac{AC}{B}$

(B) $\dfrac{AC}{100B}$

(C) $\dfrac{100B}{AC}$

(D) $\dfrac{C}{100AB}$

(E) $\dfrac{100AB}{C}$

Solving Strategy

To solve this question, we need to use the conversion factors given in the problem to convert miles per gallon to kilometers per liter, and then convert that to liters per 100 kilometers.

In some countries, gasoline is sold in liters while in other countries it is sold in gallons. Suppose that 1 gallon is equal to L liters, and 1 pound is equal to K kilogram.

Which of the following gives the volume in liters of 1,000 kilograms of gasoline whose density is D pounds per gallon?

(AMC 10A similar problem)

(A) $\dfrac{D}{KL}$

(B) $\dfrac{KL}{1,000D}$

(C) $\dfrac{1,000D}{KL}$

(D) $\dfrac{1,000L}{DK}$

(E) $\dfrac{DK}{1,000L}$

05. ■□□□□

Define $a \star b$ to be $|a + b|$ for all real numbers a and b.

What is the value of $(1 \star (2 \star -3) + ((1 \star 2) \star -3)$?

(AMC 10B problem)

(A) -3

(B) -1

(C) 0

(D) 1

(E) 3

Solving Strategy

To solve this problem, we need to understand the definition of the function $\star$ and simplify the expression.

Consider the operation "plus the reciprocal of," defined by
$$x \# y = x + \frac{1}{y}.$$

What is $((1\# - 2)\#3) + (1\#(-2\#3))$?

(AMC 10B - similar problem)

(A) $-\dfrac{1}{6}$

(B) $-\dfrac{1}{3}$

(C) 0

(D) $\dfrac{1}{3}$

(E) $\dfrac{1}{6}$

07. ◼◼◻◻

Three integers have a total sum of 96. The second integer is 40 more than the third integer, and the first integer is 6 times the third integer.

What is the absolute value of the difference between the first and second integers?

(A)   3

(B)   4

(C)   5

(D)   6

(E)   7

(AMC 10A / 12A problem)

Solving Strategy

First, use algebra to express the three integers in terms of the third integer. Then, use the fact that the sum of the three integers is 96 to solve for the third integer. Finally, substitute the value of the third integer into the expressions for the first and second integers and find the absolute value of their difference.

08. ■☐☐☐☐

The sum of three numbers is 153. The first number is 5 times the third number, and the third number is 20 less than the second number.

What is the absolute value of the difference between the second and third numbers?

(AMC 10A, 12A similar problem)

(*A*)   17

(*B*)   18

(*C*)   19

(*D*)   20

(*E*)   21

34 children visited the pastor's office on Easter and asked for Easter eggs. There are three categories: those who always tell the truth, those who always lie, and those who alternately lie and tell the truth. The alternators arbitrarily choose their first response, either a lie or the truth, but each subsequent statement has the opposite truth value from its predecessor. In the same order, the pastor asked all the children three questions.
"Are you a truth-teller?" The pastor gave an egg to each of the 23 children who answered yes.
"Are you an alternators?" The pastor gave an egg to each of the 16 children who answered yes.
"Are you a liar?" The pastor gave an egg to each of the 10 children who answered yes.

What is the total number of Easter eggs given by the pastor to the children who always tell the truth?

(AMC 10A, 12A problem)

(A)   8

(B)   9

(C)   10

(D)   11

(E)   12

⌐⌐ *Solving Strategy*

Start by identifying the number of truth-tellers, liars, and alternators.
Use the given information to form a system of equations to solve for the number of each type of child.
Use the system of equations to solve for the number of truth-tellers.

10. ▮▮▮▮▢

On Christmas, 50 children went to the mall to see Santa Claus. They can be classified into three types: Some always tell the truth; some always lie; and some alternately lie and tell the truth. The alternators arbitrarily choose their first response, either a lie or the truth, but each subsequent statement has the opposite truth value from its predecessor. Santa asked everyone the same three questions in this order.

"Are you a truth-teller?" Santa gave a gift to each of the 32 children who answered yes.

"Are you an alternator?" Santa gave a gift to each of the 22 children who answered yes.

"Are you a liar?" Santa gave a gift to each of the 14 children who answered yes.

How many gifts in all did Santa give to the children who always tell the truth?

(AMC 10A, 12A similar problem)

(A)   10

(B)   12

(C)   14

(D)   16

(E)   18

11. ◼◼☐☐☐

For how many values of the constant b will the polynomial $x^2 + bx - 48$ have two distinct integer roots?

(AMC 10B, 12B problem)

(A)   7

(B)   8

(C)   9

(D)   10

(E)   11

🔲 **Solving Strategy**

Vieta's formulas are a set of relationships between the coefficients of a polynomial and its roots. In the case of a quadratic equation of the form $ax^2 + bx + c = 0$, the formulas state that the sum of the roots is $-\frac{b}{a}$, and the product of the roots is $\frac{c}{a}$.

12.

For what integer values of k in the equation $x^2 + 3x + k = 0$ will the roots differ by less than 5?

(2022 AMC 10B - # 07, 12B - #04 similar problem)

(A)   5

(B)   6

(C)   7

(D)   8

(E)   9

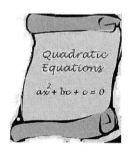

13. ■■■■□

A rectangular box (right rectangular prism) has its height, length, and width equal to the roots of the polynomial $10x^3 - 39x^2 + 29x - 6$. By adding 2 units to each edge of the original rectangular box, a new rectangular box is created.

What is the volume of the lengthening new box?

(AMC 10A, 12A problem)

(A)   18

(B)   24

(C)   30

(D)   42

(E)   56

⚙️ **Solving Strategy**

Recognize that the roots of the given polynomial correspond to the dimensions of a rectangular box. Use the formula for the volume of a rectangular box and substitute in the roots.
Find the new dimensions by adding 2 units to each dimension. Use the same formula to find the volume of the new box.

14.

The roots of the polynomial $10x^3 - 320x^2 + 3240x - 10080$ are the height, length, and width of a rectangular box (right rectangular prism). A new rectangular box is formed by shortening each edge of the original box by 2 unit.

What is the volume of the new box?

(AMC 10A, 12A similar problem)

(A) 360

(B) 480

(C) 500

(D) 520

(E) 660

15. ▓▓▓▓□□

Suppose there exists a polynomial function $f(x)$ with rational coefficients such that the remainder when $f(x)$ is divided by $x^2 - x + 1$ is $2x + 1$, and the remainder when $f(x)$ is divided by $x^2 + 1$ is $x - 2$. These two conditions uniquely determine a polynomial of the least degree.

What is the sum of the squares of coefficients of that polynomial function?

(AMC 10B, 12B problem)

(A)   33

(B)   36

(C)   39

(D)   43

(E)   46

�
⌡ **Solving Strategy**

To find the polynomial with the given properties, we use the method of setting the quotient equal to a linear term. Then, we equate the coefficients of the resulting expressions and solve for the unknown coefficients. Finally, we use the coefficients to find the polynomial and calculate the sum of the squares of the coefficients.

16. ▮▮▮☐☐

Let $f(x)$ be a polynomial function with coefficients such that when $f(x)$ is divided by the polynomial $2x^2 + x + 1$, the remainder is $x - 2$, and when $f(x)$ is divided by the polynomial $x^2 + 2$, the remainder is $3x + 1$. There is a unique polynomial of least degree with these two properties.

What is the sum of the coefficients of that polynomial?

(AMC 10B, 12B similar problem)

(A) -16

(B) -23

(C) -32

(D) $-\dfrac{121}{12}$

(E) $-\dfrac{140}{11}$

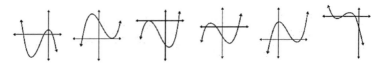

17. ▨▨▨▨▢

Mike accidentally wrote $2 \cdot \sqrt[n]{\dfrac{1}{4096}}$ instead of $2^n \cdot \sqrt{\dfrac{1}{4096}}$.

What is the value of real numbers n for which these two expressions have the same value?

(AMC 10A problem)

(A)   3

(B)   3 or 4

(C)   5

(D)   5 or 6

(E)   There are no real numbers.

Solving Strategy

To solve the problem, the first step is to convert both sides of the equation into powers of 2. Then, equate the powers of 2 on both sides and solve the resulting equation for n.

18. ■■■■■

Connie mistakenly wrote $\left(\frac{1}{3}\right)^m \cdot \sqrt[3]{\dfrac{1}{2187}}$ as $\dfrac{1}{3} \cdot \sqrt[m]{\dfrac{1}{2187}}$.

What is the sum of all real numbers m for which these two radical expressions have the same value?

(AMC 10A similar problem)

(A) $\quad -\dfrac{4}{3}$

(B) $\quad \dfrac{3}{4}$

(C) $\quad -\dfrac{1}{2}$

(D) $\quad -2$

(E) $\quad 7$

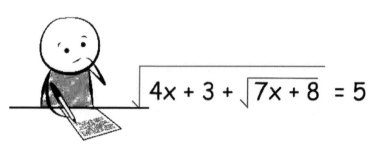

19. ■☐☐☐☐

What is the value of

$$\frac{\left(1 + \frac{1}{2}\right)\left(1 + \frac{1}{4}\right)\left(1 + \frac{1}{6}\right)}{\sqrt{\left(1 - \frac{1}{2^2}\right)\left(1 - \frac{1}{4^2}\right)\left(1 - \frac{1}{6^2}\right)}} \ ?$$

(AMC 10B problem)

(A) $\sqrt{2}$

(B) 2

(C) $\sqrt{6}$

(D) $\sqrt{7}$

(E) $2\sqrt{2}$

Solving Strategy

Difference of squares is a common algebraic expression that arises when factoring quadratic expressions. It refers to the fact that the difference between two squares can be expressed as a product of the sum and the difference of the two numbers being squared. In other words, if you have two numbers, say a and b, then the difference of squares is
$(a^2 - b^2) = (a + b)(a - b)$.

20. ■☐☐☐☐

Assume that a is a positive real number. Which is equivalent to $\sqrt{a\sqrt[3]{a}}$?

(AMC 10B similar problem)

(A) $a^{\frac{1}{2}}$

(B) $a^{\frac{1}{3}}$

(C) $a^{\frac{2}{3}}$

(D) a

(E) $a^{\frac{4}{3}}$

21.

The sum

$$\frac{1}{2!} + \frac{2}{3!} + \frac{3}{4!} + \cdots + \frac{2039}{2040!}$$

is expressed as $x - \frac{1}{y!}$, where x and y are positive integers.

What is the sum of x and y?

(AMC 10B problem)

(A)   2040

(B)   2041

(C)   2042

(D)   2043

(E)   2044

Solving Strategy

The given series can be expressed in terms of factorials, so we can use the concept of partial fractions to simplify it. Then we can use the simplified expression to find the values of x and y and calculate their sum.

22. ■☐☐☐☐

The product of all positive integers less than or equal to n can be represented using the factorial notation $n!$.

Which x makes the following equation true?
$$3 \times 5! \times 8! = 24 \times x!$$

(AMC 10B similar problem)

(A)   9

(B)   10

(C)   11

(D)   12

(E)   13

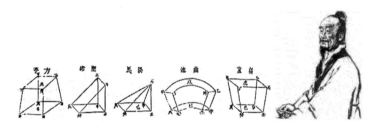

23. ■■□□□

Which expression is equivalent to

$$\left| x - 3 - \sqrt{(x - 1)^2} \right|$$

for $x < 0$?

(AMC 10A problem)

(A) $2x - 2$

(B) $2x - 4$

(C) $4 - 2x$

(D) $-2x - 4$

(E) $2x + 4$

Solving Strategy

Since the question gives the condition that x is less than 0, we know that the expression inside the absolute value will be negative. Therefore, we can simplify the expression and remove the absolute value by using the definition of absolute value that states $|a| = -a$ when a is negative.

24.

Which expression is equal to

$$\left| x - 5 + \sqrt{(x-3)^2} - \sqrt{(x-1)^2} \right|$$

for $1 < x < 3$?

(AMC 10A similar problem)

(A) $x - 1$

(B) $x + 1$

(C) $-x - 1$

(D) $-x + 1$

(E) x

25. ▮▮▮▮▯

For all real numbers x and y, let f be a function such that
$$|f(x) - f(y)| \le \frac{1}{2}|x - y|.$$

Of all such functions that also satisfy the equation $f(100) = f(700)$, what is the greatest possible value of
$$f\big(f(600)\big) - f\big(f(200)\big)?$$

(AMC 10B problem)

(A)   10

(B)   20

(C)   30

(D)   40

(E)   50

⌨ **Solving Strategy**

Start by considering the given inequality and try to manipulate it to obtain the desired expression. Don't forget to take into account the additional condition that $f(100) = f(700)$.

26. ▮▮▮▮▯

Consider functions g that satisfy

$$|g(x) - g(y)| = \frac{3}{2}|x - y|$$

for all real numbers x and y.

Of all such functions that also satisfy the equation $g(300) = g(100)$, what is the greatest possible value of

$$g(g(500)) - g(g(200))?$$

(AMC 10B similar problem)

(A)   600

(B)   625

(C)   650

(D)   675

(E)   700

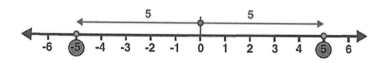

27. ▮▮▯▯▯

At 1:00 one afternoon, the mule suffers an attack of hiccups and the first hiccup occurs. Let's assume that the mule has a regular hiccup every 8 seconds.

At what time does the mule's 300th hiccup occur?

(AMC 10B problem)

(A)   1:39:44

(B)   1:39:52

(C)   1:40:08

(D)   1:41:06

(E)   1:42:00

Solving Strategy

The key to solving this problem is to recognize that the mule hiccups regularly every 8 seconds. By using this fact, you can determine the time elapsed after the first hiccup to find the time of the 300th hiccup.

28. ◼◼☐☐☐

Bella is "helping" Mama Squirrel pick up 30 acorns scattered across the floor. Bella's mother squirrel puts 3 acorns into the sack every 30 seconds, but each time immediately after those 30 seconds have elapsed, Bella takes 2 acorns out of the sack.

How many minutes will it take Bella and her mother squirrel to put all 30 acorns in the sack for the first time?

(AMC 10B similar problem)

(A)   13 *minutes* 30 *seconds*

(B)   13 *minutes* 45 *seconds*

(C)   14 *minutes*

(D)   14 *minutes* 15 *seconds*

(E)   14 *minutes* 30 *seconds*

29. ◼◼◼☐☐

The length of each side of square $PQRS$ is 1. An equilateral convex hexagon $PWXRYZ$ with side length a is formed by points W, X, Y, and Z, which lie on the sides of $PQRS$.

What is length of a?

(AMC 10A problem)

(A) $2 + \sqrt{2}$

(B) $2 - \sqrt{2}$

(C) $\dfrac{\sqrt{2}}{2}$

(D) $\dfrac{2 + \sqrt{2}}{2}$

(E) $\dfrac{2 - \sqrt{2}}{2}$

Solving Strategy

The strategy to solve this problem is to use the Pythagorean theorem and trigonometry to find the length of one of the sides of the equilateral hexagon in terms of a, and then solve for a.

30. ▮▮▮▯▯

The length of each side of square ABC is 2. Points P, Q, R, and T lie on the sides of $ABCD$, forming an equilateral convex hexagon $APQCRS$ with side length x.

What is the length of x?

(AMC 10A similar problem)

(A) $4 - 2\sqrt{2}$

(B) $4 + 2\sqrt{2}$

(C) $6 - 2\sqrt{2}$

(D) $6 + 2\sqrt{2}$

(E) $8 - 2\sqrt{2}$

31. ■■■■■

$PQRS$ is an isosceles trapezium with parallel sides $\overline{PS}$ and $\overline{QR}$, where $\overline{PS}$ is greater than $\overline{QR}$, and $\overline{PQ}$ equals $\overline{RS}$. Point X is located in the plane, and its distances from points P, Q, R, and S are $1, 2, 3$, and 4 units, respectively.

What is the value of $\dfrac{\overline{QR}}{\overline{PS}}$?

(AMC 10A, 12A problem)

(A)　$\dfrac{1}{2}$

(B)　$\dfrac{1}{3}$

(C)　$\dfrac{3}{4}$

(D)　$\dfrac{2}{5}$

(E)　$\dfrac{4}{7}$

▨ **Solving Strategy**

Reflect point X over the perpendicular bisector of QR or PS to obtain point X'. From the reflection property, use the distances given to create two new isosceles trapezoids, SPXX' and RQXX'. Recognize that opposite angles in these trapezoids are supplementary, making them cyclic quadrilaterals.

Isosceles trapezoid $WXYZ$ has parallel sides $\overline{WZ}$ and $\overline{XY}$, with $\overline{WZ} > \overline{XY}$ and $\overline{WX} = \overline{YZ}$. There is a point P inside the isosceles trapezoid such that $\overline{PW} = 2$, $\overline{PX} = 4$, $\overline{PY} = 5$, and $\overline{PZ} = 8$.

What is $\dfrac{\overline{XY}}{\overline{WZ}}$?

(AMC 10A, 12A similar problem)

(A) $\dfrac{1}{20}$

(B) $\dfrac{3}{20}$

(C) $\dfrac{7}{20}$

(D) $\dfrac{7}{30}$

(E) $\dfrac{11}{30}$

33. ▪▪▪▪☐☐

A circle can be circumscribed about quadrilateral $PQRS$ with side lengths $PQ = 7$, $QR = 24$, $RS = 20$, $SP = 15$.
The expression for the area between the circle and the quadrilateral is given by $\dfrac{x\pi - y}{z}$, where x, y, and z are positive integers with no common prime factors.

What is the value of $x + y + z$?

(AMC 10A problem)

(A)   1565

(B)   1678

(C)   1725

(D)   1818

(E)   1962

Solving Strategy

First, notice that opposite angles of a cyclic quadrilateral are supplementary. Then, use Pythagorean triple to find that PR is the diameter of the circle. Finally, use the Inscribed Angle Theorem to find the radius of the circle and calculate the area of the requested region.

34. ▮▮▮▮▯

Quadrilateral $WXYZ$ with side lengths $WX = 30$, $XY = 16$, $YZ = 14$, and a diagonal length $WY = 34$ is inscribed in a circle. The area interior to the circle but exterior to the quadrilateral can be written in the form $a\pi - b - c\sqrt{d}$, where $a, b, c,$ and d are positive integers.

What is $a + b + c + d$?

(AMC 10A similar problem)

(A) 576

(B) 600

(C) 724

(D) 815

(E) 928

35. ■■■■□

Consider the set of circles in the coordinate plane that are tangent to each of the three circles with equations $x^2 + y^2 = 4$, $x^2 + y^2 = 64$, and $(x - 5)^2 + y^2 = 3$ and denote this set as C.

What is the total area of all circles belonging to the set A?

(AMC 10B, 12B problem)

(A) 68π

(B) 84π

(C) 108π

(D) 136π

(E) 272π

Solving Strategy

We can analyze the given three circles and try to find out the common tangents of these circles. Based on the points of tangency, we can form cases and deduce the radius of the circles in the set S. Finally, we can calculate the area of all circles in S.

36. ▪▪▪▪▫

Let C be the set of circles in the coordinate plane that are tangent to each of the three circles with equations
$$x^2 + y^2 = 16, \; x^2 + y^2 = 36, \text{ and } (x + 6)^2 + y^2 = 5.$$

What is the sum of the areas of all circles in C?

(AMC 10B, 12B similar problem)

(A) 26π

(B) 52π

(C) 72π

(D) 104π

(E) 144π

37. ■■■■□

Assume that $\angle ADC$ is 42° in a rhombus $ABCD$. Consider the rhombus $ABCD$, where E is the midpoint of $\overline{CD}$ and F is the foot of the perpendicular from A to $\overline{BE}$.

What is the degree measure of $\angle BFC$?

(AMC 10B problem 20.)

(A)   109°

(B)   110°

(C)   111°

(D)   112°

(E)   113°

🔧 *Solving Strategy*

One strategy to solve this problem is to use the properties of rhombus, midpoint, and perpendicular lines. We can extend some segments and use the properties of similar triangles to find the length of some segments. Then, we can use the fact that F lies on a circle passing through A, C, and D to find the measure of angle GFC, and finally, use some angle relationships to find the measure of ∠BFC.

38. ▬▬▬▬▬▭

Let □$PQRS$ be a parallelogram with $\overline{PS} = \overline{SR}$ and angle $\angle PSR = 54°$. Let T be the midpoint of $\overline{SR}$, and let U be the point on $\overline{QT}$ such that $\overline{PU}$ is perpendicular to $\overline{QT}$.

What is the degree measure of $\angle QUR$?

(AMC 10B similar problem)

(A) 114°

(B) 115°

(C) 116°

(D) 117°

(E) 118°

Emily discovers a rectangular index card and determines that its diagonal measures 8 centimeters. Emily then removes two square pieces with side length 1 cm from opposite corners of the rectangular index card and measures the distance between the closest vertices of the two remaining corners to be $4\sqrt{2}$ cm, as shown in the diagram below.

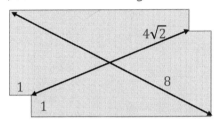

What is the total area of the rectangular index card before Emily cut out the two squares?

(AMC 10A problem)

(A) $32\sqrt{2}$

(B)   18

(C)   24

(D) $24\sqrt{2}$

(E)   64

Solving Strategy

We can use the distance formula to form equations and solve for the unknowns. Let us also imagine the figure on the rectangular coordinate plane to simplify the problem.

John has a rectangular piece of cardboard with a diagonal length of 10 cm. He cuts out two identical squares from opposite corners of the cardboard, each with side length of 1cm. He then measures the distance between the two closest vertices of these squares and finds it to be $2\sqrt{13}$ cm, as shown below.

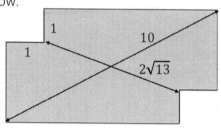

What is the area of the original cardboard?

(AMC 10A similar problem)

(A)   42

(B)   44

(C)   46

(D)   48

(E)   50

41.

Four regular hexagons of side 2 are attached to a square of side 2 to form a bowl. As illustrated in the figure, the edges of the neighboring hexagons coincide.

What is the area of the octagon formed by connecting the top eight vertices of the four hexagons located on the edge of the bowl?

(AMC 10A problem)

(A) $26\sqrt{2}$

(B) 28

(C) $30\sqrt{2}$

(D) 32

(E) $34\sqrt{2}$

To solve this problem, we can first observe that the octagon is formed by joining the eight vertices of the four hexagons situated on the rim of the bowl. We can then use the geometry of the figure to determine the lengths of the sides of the octagon and apply the formula for the area of a regular octagon.

42. ■■■□□

A bowl is formed by attaching three squares of side 2 to a equilateral triangle of side 2. The edges of the adjacent squares coincide, as shown in the figure.

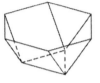

What is the area of the hexagon obtained by joining the top six vertices of the three hexagons, situated on the rim of the bowl?

(AMC 10A similar problem)

(A)   6

(B) $6\sqrt{2}$

(C) $6\sqrt{3}$

(D)   8

(E) $8\sqrt{2}$

43.

Point **X** lies on the segment $\overline{PS}$ of rhombus PQRS such that $\overline{QX}$ is perpendicular to $\overline{PS}$ and the length of $\overline{PX}$ is 6 while $\overline{XS}$ is 8.

What is the area of $\square PQRS$?

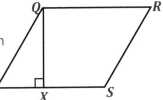

(AMC 10B problem)

(A) $40\sqrt{2}$

(B)   60

(C) $60\sqrt{2}$

(D)   80

(E) $80\sqrt{2}$

Solving Strategy

First, use the given information to find the lengths of the sides of the rhombus, and then use the formula for the area of a rhombus to find the answer.

44. ■■□□□

In isosceles trapezoid $ABCD$, point E lies on segment $\overline{AD}$ so that $\overline{BE} \perp \overline{AD}$, $AE = 5$, $BC = 15$ and $CD = 13$.

What is the area of $\square ABCD$?

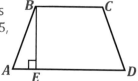

(AMC 10B similar problem)

(A)   220

(B)   240

(C)   260

(D)   280

(E)   300

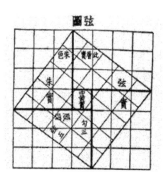

45. ▰▰▰▱▱

Consider a scalene triangle $\triangle ABC$.
Let P be a point on the $\overline{BC}$ such that the $\overline{AP}$ bisects the $\angle BAC$. Let D be the intersection of the line passing through B perpendicular to $\overline{AP}$ and the line passing through A parallel to $\overline{BC}$.

If $\overline{BP}$ has a length of 2 units and $\overline{PC}$ has a length of 3 units, what is the length of $\overline{AD}$?

(AMC 10A problem)

(A) 7

(B) 8

(C) 9

(D) 10

(E) 11

🔢 **Solving Strategy**

To solve this problem, we can use the Angle Bisector Theorem and similarity of triangles. We first bisect angle BAC using point P on line BC. Then we draw a line perpendicular to AP passing through B and intersecting the line through A parallel to BC at D. By using the Angle Bisector Theorem, we can find the length of AC, which we will need to solve for AD using similarity of triangles.

46. ▮▮▮☐☐

Consider a scalene triangle $\triangle DEF$. Point X lies on $\overline{DF}$ so that $\overline{EX}$ bisects $\angle FED$. The line through D perpendicular to $\overline{EX}$ intersects the line through D parallel to $\overline{DF}$ at point G. Suppose $\overline{DX} = 4$ and $\overline{FX} = 5$.

What is EG?

(AMC 10A similar problem)

(A)   16

(B)   20

(C)   24

(D)   30

(E)   36

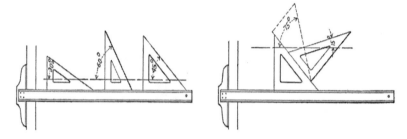

47.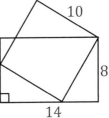

The diagram below shows a rectangle with side lengths 8 and 14 and a square with side length 10.
As shown, the square is positioned such that three of its vertices lie on three different sides of the rectangle.

What is the area of the overlap between the square and the rectangle?

(AMC 10B, 12B problem)

(A)   42.5

(B)   62.5

(C)   82

(D)   82.5

(E)   102

Solving Strategy

First, use angle chasing to determine the similarity of triangles. Then use the given side lengths of the rectangle and square to determine the lengths of the sides of these triangles. Finally, use the areas of these triangles to find the area of the region inside both the square and rectangle

48. ■■☐☐☐

All of the triangles in the diagram
below are similar to isosceles triangle
PQR, in which $PQ = PR$.
Each of the 9 smallest triangles has
area 1, and triangle PQR has area 50.

What is the area of trapezoid $QSTR$?

(AMC 10B, 12B similar problem)

(A)   10

(B)   15

(C)   20

(D)   25

(E)   30

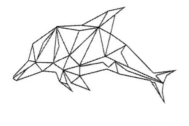
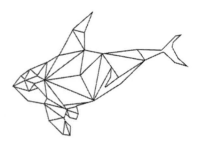

In a 5×5 grid, every square can be either empty or filled and has a maximum of eight neighboring squares that share a side or a corner. The following rules are used to transform the grid:

① A square that is filled will remain filled if it has two or three filled neighboring squares.

② An empty square will be filled if it has exactly three filled neighbors.

③ Squares that are not filled and do not have exactly three filled neighbors remain empty.

An example of the grid transformation is illustrated in the figure below.

[before]　　　　transformation　　　　[after]

Assuming that there is a 3×3 subgrid at the center of a 5×5 grid, the remaining squares in the grid form an empty border around it. What is the number of initial configurations that will result in a transformed grid containing only one filled square at the center after a single transformation?

(Different configurations obtained by rotating or reflecting a configuration are considered as distinct.)

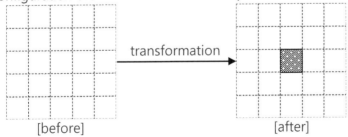

[before]　　　　transformation　　　　[after]

(2022 AMC 10B problem 19, 12B problem 18.)

continue on the next page 👉

(A) 14 (B) 16 (C) 18 (D) 20 (E) 22

50. ■■□□□

If point $P = (4,3)$ is rotated $90°$ clockwise about the origin, it will result in point P'. Point P'' is the image of point P' under reflection across the x-axis.

What is the distance between P and P''?

(AMC 10B, 12B similar problem)

(A) 5

(B) $5\sqrt{2}$

(C) 7

(D) $7\sqrt{2}$

(E) 10

51. ■■■□□

R_k is a transformation of the coordinate plane that involves a counterclockwise rotation of n degrees around the origin followed by a reflection of the plane over the y-axis.

What is the smallest positive integer value of n for which applying the transformations R_1, R_2, R_3, ..., R_n sequentially results in the point $(1,0)$ returning to its original position?

(AMC 10A, 12A problem)

(A)   179

(B)   180

(C)   181

(D)   359

(E)   360

Solving Strategy

The strategy is to first analyze the transformation R and its two steps, rotating the plane counterclockwise by n degrees around the origin and then reflecting across the y-axis. Next, we need to find the pattern of angles at which the point $(1,0)$ ends up after each transformation $R_1, R_2, R_3, ... R_n$. Finally, we need to find the least positive integer n such that performing the sequence of transformations returns the point $(1,0)$ back to itself, which means that the final angle should be 0 degrees.

52.

Let T_k be the transformation of the coordinate plane that first reflects the plane across the x-axis and then rotates the plane k degrees counterclockwise around the origin.

What is the smallest positive integer n such that applying the transformations T_1, T_2, $T_3, \ldots, T_n$ sequentially returns the point $(1,1)$ back to its original position?

(AMC 10A, 12A similar problem)

(A)   179

(B)   180

(C)   181

(D)   359

(E)   360

Translation

Rotation

Reflection

Enlargement

Question	Answer	Question	Answer
01.	B	27.	B
02.	A	28.	C
03.	E	29.	B
04.	D	30.	A
05.	E	31.	B
06.	E	32.	B
07.	C	33.	A
08.	D	34.	B
09.	A	35.	D
10.	C	36.	D
11.	D	37.	C
12.	B	38.	D
13.	C	39.	B
14.	B	40.	D
15.	A	41.	B
16.	E	42.	C
17.	B	43.	D
18.	A	44.	B
19.	D	45.	D
20.	C	46.	E
21.	B	47.	B
22.	B	48.	D
23.	C	49.	E
24.	B	50.	D
25.	E	51.	D
26.	D	52.	A

01. **Answer** (B)

Let's start by using a proportion to find the speed at which Albert cycled. We know that he completed 15 laps in 57 minutes, so his average speed was:

speed = distance/time = $\frac{15\ laps}{57\ minutes} = \frac{5\ laps}{19\ mins}$

Now we can use this speed to find the number of laps he completed in the first 27 minutes.
We can set up a proportion:

$$\frac{5\ laps}{19\ minutes} = \frac{x\ laps}{27\ minutes}$$

To solve for x, we can cross-multiply:

$$19x = 5 \times 27 \quad \rightarrow \quad x = \frac{135}{9} \approx 7.11$$

Therefore, he completed approximately 7 laps.

02. **Answer** (A)

Let's start by finding John's running speed. We know that he can run 10 laps around a track in 30 minutes, so his speed is:

speed = distance/time = $\frac{10\ laps}{30\ minutes} = \frac{1}{3}$ lap per minutes

Now, we need to find the number of laps John ran in the first 12 minutes. We can use the ratio of his speed and time:
number of laps = speed x time
= (1/3 lap per minute) x 12 minutes = 4 laps

Therefore, John ran 4 laps in the first 12 minutes.

03. **Answer** (E)

We are given that 1 kilometer equals A miles and 1 gallon equals B liters. To convert C miles per gallon to kilometers per liter, we need to first convert miles to kilometers and gallons to liters.

1 kilometer = A miles
1 gallon = B liters
C miles = $\frac{C}{A}$ kilometers ($\leftarrow \frac{1\ km}{A\ mile} = \frac{?\ km}{C\ mile}$)

So, the fuel efficiency in kilometers per liter is:

$$\frac{C \ miles}{1 \ gallon} \ \rightarrow \ \frac{\frac{C}{A} \ kilometer}{B \ liters} = \frac{C}{AB} \ kilometer \ per \ liter$$

To convert this to liters per 100 kilometers,
first, finding the reciprocal of fuel efficiency in kilometers per liter;

$$\frac{C}{AB} \ kilometer \ per \ liter \ \rightarrow \ \frac{AB}{C} liters \ per \ kilometer$$

this means that automobile needs $\frac{AB}{C}$ liters of fuel to travel 1 km.

so, the efficiency of the car for 100 km can be obtained by multiplying the above value by 100

$$\frac{AB}{C} \times 100 = \frac{100AB}{C}$$

Therefore, the fuel efficiency in liters per 100 kilometers for a car that gets x miles per gallon is $\frac{100AB}{C}$.

<table><tr><td>04.</td><td>Answer</td><td>(D)</td></tr></table>

We are given that 1 gallon equals L liters and 1 pound equals K kilograms. To convert D pounds per gallon to kilograms per liter, we need to first convert pounds to kilograms and gallons to liters.

1 pound = K kilograms
1 gallon = L liters

D pounds = DK kilograms $(\leftarrow \frac{1 \ pound}{K \ kilograms} = \frac{D \ pounds}{? \ kilograms})$

So, the density in kilograms per liter is:

$$\frac{D \ pounds}{1 \ gallon} \ \rightarrow \ \frac{DK \ kilograms}{L \ liters} = \frac{DK}{L} \ kilograms \ per \ liter$$

And then,
finding the reciprocal of density in liters per kilograms;

$$\frac{DK}{L} \ kilograms \ per \ liter \ \rightarrow \ \frac{L}{DK} liters \ per \ kilograms$$

this means that the volume in liter of 1kg is $\frac{L}{DK}$ liters.

So, the volume in liters of 1,000 kilograms of gasoline is;

$$\frac{L}{DK} \times 1000 = \frac{1000L}{DK}.$$

Answer **(E)**

First, let's use the definition of ☆ to simplify the expression inside the parentheses:
$$2 ☆ -3 = |2 + (-3)| = 1$$
$$(1 ☆ (2 ☆ -3) = 1 ☆ 1 = |1 + 1| = 2$$

Next, let's simplify the expression outside the parentheses:
$$1 ☆ 2 = |1 + 2| = 3$$
$$((1 ☆ 2) ☆ -3) = 3 ☆ -3 = |3 + (-3)| = 0$$

Finally, substituting these values into the original expression, we get:
$$(1 ☆ (2 ☆ -3) + ((1 ☆ 2) ☆ -3) = 3 + 0 = 3$$

Therefore, the value of the expression is 3.

---

06. **Answer** **(E)**

First, let's use the definition of ☆ to simplify the expression inside the parentheses:
$$-2 = 1 + \frac{1}{-2} = \frac{1}{2}$$
$$((1\# - 2)\#3) = \frac{1}{2}\#3 = \frac{1}{2} + \frac{1}{3} = \frac{5}{6}$$

Next, let's simplify the expression outside the parentheses:
$$-2\#3 = -2 + \frac{1}{3} = -\frac{5}{3}$$
$$(1\#(-2\#3) = 1\# - \frac{5}{3} = 1 + \left(-\frac{5}{3}\right) = -\frac{2}{3}$$

Finally, substituting these values into the original expression, we get:
$$\frac{5}{6} + \left(-\frac{2}{3}\right) = \frac{1}{6}$$

07. *Answer*   (**C**)

Let N be the third integer. Then, the second integer is $N + 40$ and the first integer is $6N$.
The sum of the three integers is 96, so we can write the equation:
$$6N + N + 40 + N = 96$$

Simplifying this equation, we get $8N = 56$, so $N = 7$.
Substituting $N = 7$ into the expressions for the first and second integers,
we get $6N = 42$ and $N + 40 = 47$.

Therefore, the absolute value of the difference between the first and second integers is $|42 - 47| = 5$.

08. *Answer*   (**D**)

Let the third number be x. From the second statement, we know that the second number is $x + 20$. Using the fact that the sum of the three numbers is 150, we can write:
$$5x + (x + 20) + x = 153$$

Simplifying and solving for x, we get:
$$x = 19$$

Substituting $x = 19$ into the expressions for the second and third numbers, we get:
second number: $19 + 20 = 19 + 20 = 39$

Therefore, the absolute value of the difference between the second and third numbers is: $|39 - 19| = 20$

The problem provides information about the number of children who always tell the truth, always lie, and alternate between truth and lies. We need to determine the number of truth-tellers and the total number of eggs given to them.

Let T be the number of truth-tellers, L be the number of liars, A be the number of alternators who answered yes-no-yes, and A' be the number of alternators who answered no-yes-no.

① There are total 34 children.
$$T + L + A + A' = 34$$

② For the third question, the pastor asked if they were liars. Those who always tell the truth said "no" and those who always lie said "no" too, but they were lying. Only the alternaters who lie would answer "yes" to this question. All of the 10 children who answered "yes" are alternaters who lied on Questions 1 and 3 (they said "yes" then "no" then "yes"). The other alternaters, who answered "no" to the third question, have the opposite behavior. If we call A as the number of alternaters who answered yes-no-yes, and A' as the number of alternaters who answered no-yes-no, then A equals 10.
$$A = 10$$

③ For the second question, the pastor asked if the children were alternaters. The children who always tell the truth would say "no," and the liars would say "yes." However, the alternaters who answered "no-yes-no" would also say "yes." In total, 16 children (the liars and the "no-yes-no" alternaters) answered "yes."
$$L + A' = 16$$

④ The first question asked by the pastor was, "Are you a truth teller?" The children who always tell the truth answered "yes," and the children who always lie also answered "yes." The children who alternately lie and tell the truth answered "yes" if they started with a lie and "no" if they started with the truth. Therefore, the total number of children who answered "yes" to this question was the sum of the number of truth-tellers, liars, and alternaters who answered "yes," which is 23.
$$T + L + A = 23$$

So,
$$T + L + A + A' = 23 + A' = 34 \quad \rightarrow \quad A' = 11$$
$$L + A' = L + 11 = 16 \quad \rightarrow \quad L = 5$$
$$T + 5 + 10 + 11 = 34 \quad \rightarrow \quad T = 8$$

Therefore, the total number of Easter eggs given by the pastor to the children who always tell the truth is 8.

10. **Answer** **(C)**

Let T be the number of truth-tellers, L be the number of liars, A be the number of alternators who answered yes-no-yes, and A' be the number of alternators who answered no-yes-no. Then we have:
① There are total 50 children.
  $T + L + A + A' = 50$ (1)
② From the first question
  $T + L + A = 32$ (2)
③ From the second question
  $L + A' = 22$ (3)
④ From the third question
  $A = 14$ (4)

From (4), we know that there are 22 alternators who answered yes-no-yes A=14. From (1) and (2) A'=18, so L=4 and T=14.

Therefore, there 14 children who always tell the truth.

11. **Answer** **(D)**

Let the roots of the polynomial $x^2 + bx - 48$ be p and q, where p and q are distinct integers.
Then, by Vieta's formulas, we have:
$$p + q = -b \quad and \quad pq = -48.$$

Since p and q are distinct integers, they must be two distinct factors of 48. Therefore, the possibilities for p and q are
  $(\pm 1, \mp 48), (\pm 2, \mp 24), (\pm 3, \mp 16), (\pm 4, \mp 12) \ and \ (\pm 6, \mp 8).$

For each pair of values for p and q, we can find the corresponding value of b by using the equation $p + q = -b$
For example,
if $p = 1$ and $q = -48$, then $b = 1 + (-48) = -47 \rightarrow b = 47$.
Using this method, we can find 10 values of b that satisfy the conditions.

Therefore, there are 10 possible values of b in total.

12. **Answer** (**B**)

Let the roots of the equation $x^2 + 3x + k = 0$ be p and q.
Using the quadratic formula, we can express p and q as:

$$p = \frac{-3 + \sqrt{9 - 4k}}{2}, \qquad q = \frac{-3 - \sqrt{9 - 4k}}{2}$$

For the difference between the roots to be less than 5, we need;

$$p - q = \sqrt{9 - 4k} < 5.$$

Take square on both side;

$$9 - 4k < 25 \quad \rightarrow \quad k > -4.$$

And, inside square root is never negative, so

$$9 - 4k \geq 0 \quad \rightarrow \quad k \leq \frac{9}{4}(= 2.25).$$

Therefore, the possible value of k is;

$$-3, \quad -2, \quad -1, \quad 0, \quad 1, \quad 2.$$

13. **Answer** (**C**)

The given polynomial, $10x^3 - 39x^2 + 29x - 6$, has three roots, which correspond to the height, length, and width of a rectangular box. Let's call these roots a, b, and c.
To find the volume of the new box, we need to lengthen each edge by 2 units. This means that the new dimensions are $(a + 2)$, $(b + 2)$, and $(c + 2)$.
Therefore, the volume of the new box is $V = (a + 2)(b + 2)(c + 2)$.

Expanding this expression, we get

$$V = abc + 2(ac + ab + bc) + 4(a + b + c) + 8.$$

To find the values of $ab + ac + bc$, abc, and $a + b + c$,
use the given polynomial is equal to $10(x - a)(x - b)(x - c)$.
Expanding this expression gives us

$$\begin{aligned}
10x^3 &- 39x^2 + 29x - 6 \\
&= 10(x - a)(x - b)(x - c) \\
&= 10x^3 - 10(a + b + c)x^2 + 10(ab + ac + bc)x - 10abc.
\end{aligned}$$

Comparing coefficients,
we get $ab + ac + bc = \frac{29}{10}$, $abc = \frac{6}{10}$, and $a + b + c = \frac{39}{10}$.
Substituting these values into the expression for V,
we get $V = \frac{6}{10} + 2\left(\frac{29}{10}\right) + 4\left(\frac{39}{10}\right) + 8 = 30$.

Therefore, the volume of the new box is 30 cubic units.

14. **Answer** (B)

The given polynomial, $10x^3 - 320x^2 + 3240x - 10080$, has three roots, which correspond to the height, length, and width of a rectangular box. Let's call these roots a, b, and c.
To find the volume of the new box, we need to shorten each edge by 2 units. This means that the new dimensions are $(a - 2)$, $(b - 2)$, and $(c - 2)$.
Therefore, the volume of the new box is $V = (a - 2)(b - 2)(c - 2)$.

Expanding this expression, we get
$$V = abc - 2(ac + ab + bc) + 4(a + b + c) - 8.$$

To find the values of $ab + ac + bc$, abc, and $a + b + c$,
use the given polynomial is equal to $8(x - a)(x - b)(x - c)$.
Expanding this expression gives us
$$10x^3 - 320x^2 + 3240x - 10080$$
$$= 10(x - a)(x - b)(x - c)$$
$$= 10x^3 - 10(a + b + c)x^2 + 10(ab + ac + bc)x - 10abc.$$

Comparing coefficients,
we get $a + b + c = 32$, $ab + ac + bc = 324$ and $abc = 1008$.

Substituting these values into the expression for V,
we get $V = 1008 - 2(324) + 4(32) - 8 = 480$.

Therefore, the volume of the new box is 480 cubic units.

15. **Answer** (A)

Let $f(x) = (x^2 - x + 1)(ax + b) + (2x + 1)$
and $f(x) = (x^2 + 1)(ax + c) + (x - 2)$.

Expanding both equations;
$$f(x) = ax^3 + (-a + b)x^2 + (a - b + 2)x + (b + 1) \text{ and}$$
$$f(x) = ax^3 + cx^2 + (a + 1)x + (c - 2).$$

Since $f(x)$ has the same coefficients and the constant in both cases; $-a + b = c$, $a - b + 2 = a + 1$, and $b + 1 = c - 2$.
So,
$$b = 1, c = 4, \text{ and } a = -3.$$

Therefore the polynomial function is
$$f(x) = -3x^3 + 4x^2 - 2x + 2 \text{ and}$$
the sum of the squares of the coefficients of $f(x)$ is
$$(-3)^2 + (4)^2 + (-2)^2 + 2^2 = 33.$$

16.	**Answer**	(**E**)

Let $f(x) = (2x^2 + x + 1)(ax + b) + (x - 2)$
and $f(x) = (x^2 + 2)(2ax + c) + (3x + 1)$.

Expanding both equations;
$$f(x) = 2ax^3 + (a + 2b)x^2 + (a + b + 1)x + (b - 2) \text{ and }$$
$$f(x) = 2ax^3 + cx^2 + (4a + 3)x + (2c + 1).$$

Since $f(x)$ has the same coefficients and the constant in both cases; $a + 2b = c$, $a + b + 1 = 4a + 3$, and $b - 1 = 2c + 1$.
So,
$$a = -\frac{9}{11}, \qquad b = -\frac{5}{11} \quad and \quad c = -\frac{19}{11}$$

Therefore the polynomial function is
$$f(x) = -\frac{18}{11}x^3 - \frac{19}{11}x^2 - \frac{76}{11}x - \frac{27}{11}$$
and the sum of the squares of the coefficients of $f(x)$ is
$$-\frac{18}{11} + \left(-\frac{19}{11}\right) + \left(-\frac{76}{11}\right) + \left(-\frac{27}{11}\right) = -\frac{140}{11}$$

17.	**Answer**	(**B**)

Given, $2\sqrt[n]{\dfrac{1}{4096}} = 2^n \sqrt{\dfrac{1}{4096}}$.

Rewrite the equation by powers of 2;
$$2 \cdot (2^{-12})^{\frac{1}{n}} = 2^n \cdot (2^{-12})^{\frac{1}{2}}$$
$$\rightarrow 2^{1-\frac{12}{n}} = 2^{n-6} \quad \rightarrow \quad 1 - \frac{12}{n} = n - 6$$
Multiply both sides by n;
$$n - 12 = n^2 - 6n \quad \rightarrow \quad n^2 - 7n + 12 = 0$$

Solve the quadratic equation for n;
$$n^2 - 7n + 12 = 0 \quad \rightarrow \quad (n - 3)(n - 4) = 0$$
$$\rightarrow n = 3 \ or \ n = 4$$

Therefore, the value of real numbers n is 3 or 4.

18. *Answer*   **(A)**

Given, $\left(\frac{1}{3}\right)^m \sqrt[3]{\frac{1}{2187}} = \left(\frac{1}{3}\right)^m \sqrt[m]{\frac{1}{2187}}$

Rewrite the equation by powers of 3;

$$3^{-m} \cdot (3^{-7})^{\frac{1}{3}} = 3^{-1} \cdot (3^{-7})^{\frac{1}{m}}$$

$$\rightarrow 3^{-m-\frac{7}{3}} = 3^{-1-\frac{7}{m}} \quad \rightarrow \quad -m - \frac{7}{3} = -1 - \frac{7}{m}$$

Multiply both sides by $3m$;

$$-3m^2 - 7m = -3m - 21 \quad \rightarrow \quad -3m^2 - 4m + 21 = 0$$

The sum of roots of a quadratic equation $ax^2 + bx + c = 0$ can be found without actually calculating the roots and the sum is $-\frac{b}{a}$.

So,

the sum of all real numbers m for the equation is

$$-\frac{b}{a} = -\frac{-4}{-3} = -\frac{4}{3}.$$

Therefore, the sum of all real numbers m is $-\frac{4}{3}$.

19. *Answer*   **(D)**

We apply the difference of squares to the denominator, and then regroup factors:

$$\frac{\left(1+\frac{1}{2}\right)\left(1+\frac{1}{4}\right)\left(1+\frac{1}{6}\right)}{\sqrt{\left(1-\frac{1}{2^2}\right)\left(1-\frac{1}{4^2}\right)\left(1-\frac{1}{6^2}\right)}}$$

$$= \frac{\left(1+\frac{1}{2}\right)\left(1+\frac{1}{4}\right)\left(1+\frac{1}{6}\right)}{\sqrt{\left(1+\frac{1}{2}\right)\left(1+\frac{1}{4}\right)\left(1+\frac{1}{6}\right)}\sqrt{\left(1-\frac{1}{2}\right)\left(1-\frac{1}{4}\right)\left(1-\frac{1}{6}\right)}}$$

$$= \frac{\sqrt{\left(1+\frac{1}{2}\right)\left(1+\frac{1}{4}\right)\left(1+\frac{1}{6}\right)}}{\sqrt{\left(1-\frac{1}{2}\right)\left(1-\frac{1}{4}\right)\left(1-\frac{1}{6}\right)}}$$

$$= \frac{\sqrt{\frac{3}{2} \times \frac{5}{4} \times \frac{7}{6}}}{\sqrt{\frac{1}{2} \times \frac{3}{4} \times \frac{5}{6}}} = \frac{\sqrt{3 \times 5 \times 7}}{\sqrt{1 \times 3 \times 5}} = \sqrt{7}$$

20. **Answer** **(C)**

We can start by using the Law of Exponents to simplify the given expression:

$$\sqrt{a\sqrt[3]{a}} = \sqrt{a^{\frac{4}{3}}} = \left(a^{\frac{4}{3}}\right)^{\frac{1}{2}} = a^{\frac{2}{3}}.$$

21. **Answer** **(B)**

We can use the concept of partial fractions to express the given series in terms of factorials.

Using the partial fraction decomposition, we get:

$$\frac{n}{(n+1)!} = \frac{a}{n!} + \frac{b}{(n+1)!}$$
$$= \frac{a \times (n+1)! + b \times n!}{n! \times (n+1)!}$$
$$= \frac{an + a + b}{(n+1)!}$$

so, $a = 1$, $b = -1$ and

$$\frac{n}{(n+1)!} = \frac{1}{n!} - \frac{1}{(n+1)!}$$

So, the given series can be written as:

$$\frac{1}{2!} + \frac{2}{3!} + \frac{3}{4!} + \dots + \frac{2039}{2040!}$$
$$= \left(\frac{1}{1!} - \frac{1}{2!}\right) + \left(\frac{1}{2!} - \frac{1}{3!}\right) + \left(\frac{1}{3!} - \frac{1}{4!}\right) + \dots + \left(\frac{1}{2039!} - \frac{1}{2040!}\right)$$
$$= \frac{1}{1!} - \frac{1}{2040!}$$
$$= 1 - \frac{1}{2040!}$$

Now, we can see that $x = 1$ and $y = 2040$, so $x + y = 2041$.

22. **Answer** **(B)**

We have $6! = 1 \times 2 \times 3 \times 4 \times 5 \times 6$, so we can rewrite $3 \times 6! \times 8!$ as follows:

$$3 \times 6! \times 8! = 3 \times 3 \times 2 \times 5 \times 4 \times 6 \times 8!$$
$$= 24 \times 8! \times 9 \times 10$$
$$= 24 \times 10!$$

Therefore, the value of x that satisfies the equation is 10.

23. **Answer** (**C**)

Since we know that $x < 0 < 1$, we can simplify the expression by replacing $\sqrt{(x-1)^2}$ with $-(x-1)$.

So,

$$\left| x - 3 - \sqrt{(x-1)^2} \right| = \left| x - 3 - \left(-(x-1)\right) \right|$$
$$= \left| x - 3 + (x-1) \right|$$
$$= \left| x - 3 + x - 1 \right|$$
$$= \left| 2x - 4 \right|$$

the absolute value is never negative ($|x| \geq 0$) and $2x < 0 < 4$.

Therefore, equivalent expression is $-(2x-4) = 4 - 2x$.

24. **Answer** (**B**)

Since we know that $1 < x < 3$, we can simplify the expression by replacing $\sqrt{(x-3)^2}$ with $-(x-3)$ and $\sqrt{(x-1)^2}$ with $(x-1)$.

So,

$$\left| x - 5 + \sqrt{(x-3)^2} - \sqrt{(x-1)^2} \right|$$
$$= \left| x - 5 + \left(-(x-3)\right) - (x-1) \right|$$
$$= \left| x - 5 - x + 3 - x + 1 \right|$$
$$= \left| -x - 1 \right|$$
$$= \left| -x - 1 \right|$$

the absolute value is never negative.

Therefore, equivalent expression is $-(-x-1) = x + 1$.

Let's consider the given inequality:

$$|f(x) - f(y)| \le \frac{1}{2}|x - y|$$

Use this inequality to obtain bounds for $|f(f(600)) - f(f(200))|$:

$$|f(f(600)) - f(f(200))| \le \frac{1}{2}|f(600) - f(200)|$$

$$\le \frac{1}{2}|\frac{1}{2}|600 - 200||$$

$$\le 100$$

So, $-100 \le f(f(600)) - f(f(200)) \le 100$ (1).

Now, we need to take into account the additional condition and let be $f(100) = f(700) = c$.

$$|f(600) - f(100)| \le \frac{1}{2}|600 - 100|$$

$$\le 250$$

$$|f(600) - f(700)| \le \frac{1}{2}|600 - 700|$$

$$\le 50$$

so, $|f(600) - c| \le 50 \quad \rightarrow \quad -50 \le f(600) - c \le 50$.

$$|f(200) - f(700)| \le \frac{1}{2}|200 - 700|$$

$$\le 250$$

$$|f(200) - f(100)| \le \frac{1}{2}|200 - 100|$$

$$\le 50$$

so, $|f(200) - c| \le 50 \quad \rightarrow \quad -50 \le f(200) - c \le 50$.

Using above condition:

$$|f(f(600)) - f(f(200))| \le \frac{1}{2}|f(600) - f(200)|$$

$$\le \frac{1}{2}|(f(600) - c) - (f(200) - c)|$$

$$\le \frac{1}{2}|50 - (-50)|$$

$$\le 50$$

So, $-50 \le f(f(600)) - f(f(200)) \le 50$ (2).

The value of $f(f(600)) - f(f(200))$ satisfy (1) and (2) conditions. Therefore, the maximum value is 50.

Let's consider the given inequality:

$$|g(x) - g(y)| \le \frac{3}{2}|x - y|$$

Use this inequality to obtain bounds for $|g(g(500)) - g(g(200))|$:

$$|g(g(500)) - g(g(200))| \le \frac{3}{2}|g(500) - g(200)|$$
$$\le \frac{3}{2}|\frac{3}{2}|500 - 200||$$
$$\le 675$$

So, $-675 \le g(g(500)) - g(g(200)) \le 675$ (1).

Now, we need to take into account the additional condition and let be $g(300) = g(100) = c$.

$$|g(500) - g(100)| \le \frac{3}{2}|500 - 100|$$
$$\le 600$$
$$|g(500) - g(300)| \le \frac{3}{2}|500 - 300|$$
$$\le 300$$

so, $|g(500) - c| \le 300 \quad \rightarrow \quad -300 \le g(500) - c \le 300$.

$$|g(200) - g(300)| \le \frac{3}{2}|200 - 300|$$
$$\le 150$$
$$|g(200) - g(100)| \le \frac{3}{2}|200 - 100|$$
$$\le 150$$

so, $|g(200) - c| \le 150 \quad \rightarrow \quad -150 \le g(200) - c \le 150$.

Using above condition:

$$|g(g(500)) - g(g(200))| \le \frac{3}{2}|g(500) - g(200)|$$
$$\le \frac{3}{2}|(g(500) - c) - (g(200) - c)|$$
$$\le \frac{3}{2}|300 - (-150)|$$
$$\le 675$$

So, $-675 \le f(f(600)) - f(f(200)) \le 675$.

Therefore, the maximum value is 675.

27.	Answer	(B)

Since the mule hiccups every 8 seconds, the time elapsed after the first hiccup is 8 seconds for the second hiccup, 16 seconds for the third hiccup, and so on.

The time elapsed after the $(n-1)$th hiccup is $8 \times (n-1)$ seconds. To find the time of the 300th hiccup, we need to calculate the time elapsed after the 299th hiccup:
Time elapsed after the 299th hiccup is
$$8 \times (300-1) \; seconds \; = \; 2392 \; seconds.$$

Adding 2392 seconds to the time of the first hiccup (which occurred at 1:00), we get:
$$1:00 + 2392 \sec = 1 + 39\min + 52\sec = \; 1:39:52.$$

Therefore, the 300th hiccup occurs at 1:39:52.

28.	Answer	(C)

Every 30 seconds, 3 acorns are put in the box and 2 toys are taken out, so the number of acorns in the box increases by 3-2=1 every 30 seconds.
Then after $(27) \times (30) = 810$ seconds (or 13.5 minutes), there are 27 acorns in the box. Bella's mom will then put the remaining 3 acorns into the box after 30 more seconds, so the total time taken is $27 \times 30 + 30 = 840$ seconds, or 14 minutes.

Note: During the last time Bella's mom will complete picking up the 30 acorns(before Bella can take 2 out) which is the reason that you calculate up to 27 and then the rest.

Let's label the points
where the hexagon intersects the sides of the
square as follows:

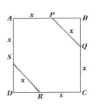

Since the hexagon is equilateral, all its sides have
length a. Let's consider triangle QWX. This is an
isosceles right triangle with legs of length $1 - a$,
so finding hypotenuse WX (a) by the Pythagorean theorem;

$$(1 - a)^2 + (1 - a)^2 = a^2$$
$$\rightarrow a^2 = 2(1 - a)^2 \quad \rightarrow \quad a = \sqrt{2}(1 - a)$$
$$\rightarrow a = \sqrt{2} - \sqrt{2}a \quad \rightarrow \quad a + \sqrt{2}a = \sqrt{2}$$
$$\rightarrow a = \frac{\sqrt{2}}{\sqrt{2} + 1} \quad \rightarrow \quad a = \frac{\sqrt{2}}{\sqrt{2} + 1} \times \frac{\sqrt{2} - 1}{\sqrt{2} - 1} = \frac{2 - \sqrt{2}}{2 - 1}$$

Therefore, the length of a is $2 - \sqrt{2}$.

30. **Answer** (A)

Let's label the points
where the hexagon intersects the sides of the
square as follows:

Since the hexagon is equilateral, all its sides have
length x. Let's consider triangle BPQ. This is an
isosceles right triangle with legs of length $2 - x$.
so finding hypotenuse PQ (x) by the Pythagorean theorem;

$$(2 - x)^2 + (2 - x)^2 = x^2$$
$$\rightarrow x^2 = 2(2 - x)^2 \quad \rightarrow \quad x = \sqrt{2}(2 - x)$$
$$\rightarrow x = 2\sqrt{2} - \sqrt{2}x \quad \rightarrow \quad (\sqrt{2} + 1) = 2\sqrt{2}$$
$$\rightarrow x = \frac{2\sqrt{2}}{\sqrt{2} + 1} \quad \rightarrow \quad x = \frac{2\sqrt{2}}{\sqrt{2} + 1} \times \frac{\sqrt{2} - 1}{\sqrt{2} - 1} = \frac{4 - 2\sqrt{2}}{2 - 1}$$

Therefore, the length of a is $4 - 2\sqrt{2}$.

To solve the problem, first reflect point X over the perpendicular bisector of QR or PS to obtain point X'. We can then use the distances given to create two new isosceles trapezoids, $SPXX'$ and $RQXX'$, as shown in the diagram below.

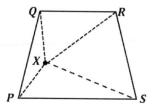 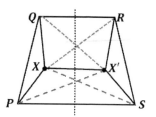

Since a perpendicular bisector of XX', PS and QR, opposite angles in these trapezoids are supplementary, making them cyclic quadrilaterals. We can then apply Ptolemy's theorem to both trapezoids to obtain expressions for the lengths of XX', QR, and PS.

In $SPXX'$,
we have $\overline{XX'} \times \overline{PS} + \overline{XP} \times \overline{X'S} = \overline{PX} \times \overline{SX'}$. Substituting the given values, we get $\overline{XX'} \times \overline{PS} + 1 \times 1 = 4 \times 4$, which simplifies to
$$\overline{XX'} \times \overline{PS} = 15.$$

In $RQXX'$,
we have $\overline{XX'} \times \overline{QR} + \overline{QX} \times \overline{RX'} = \overline{QX'} \times \overline{RX}$. Substituting the given values, we get $\overline{XX'} \times \overline{QR} + 2 \times 2 = 3 \times 3$, which simplifies to
$$\overline{XX'} \times \overline{QR} = 5.$$

Therefore, the value of $\dfrac{\overline{QR}}{\overline{PS}}$ is
$$\frac{(\overline{XX'} \times \overline{QR})}{\overline{XX'} \times \overline{PS}} = \frac{5}{15} = \frac{1}{3}.$$

To solve the problem, first reflect point P over the perpendicular bisector of XY or WZ to obtain point P'. We can then use the distances given to create two new isosceles trapezoids, $WPP'Z$ and $XPP'Y$, as shown in the diagram below.

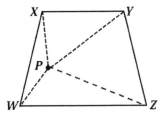 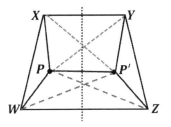

Since a perpendicular bisector of both PP', XY and WZ, opposite angles in these trapezoids are supplementary, making them cyclic quadrilaterals. We can then apply Ptolemy's theorem to both trapezoids to obtain expressions for the lengths of PP', XY, and WZ.

In $WPP'Z$,
we have $\overline{PP'} \times \overline{WZ} + \overline{PW} \times \overline{P'Z} = \overline{PZ} \times \overline{P'X}$. Substituting the given values, we get $\overline{PP'} \times \overline{WZ} + 2 \times 2 = 8 \times 8$, which simplifies to
$$\overline{PP'} \times \overline{WZ} = 60.$$

In $XPP'Y$,
we have $\overline{PP'} \times \overline{XY} + \overline{PX} \times \overline{P'Y} = \overline{PY} \times \overline{P'X}$. Substituting the given values, we get $\overline{PP'} \times \overline{XY} + 4 \times 4 = 5 \times 5$, which simplifies to
$$\overline{PP'} \times \overline{XY} = 9.$$

Therefore, the value of $\dfrac{\overline{XY}}{\overline{WZ}}$ is

$$\frac{\overline{PP'} \times \overline{XY}}{\overline{PP'} \times \overline{WZ}} = \frac{9}{60} = \frac{3}{20}.$$

Answer (*A*)

Quadrilateral PQRS is a cyclic quadrilateral and opposite angles of every cyclic quadrilateral are supplementary.
So, $\angle Q + \angle S = 180$.

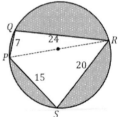

We claim that PR=25. We try to prove it by contradiction.

① Assume that AC<25.
   Then, triangles PQR and PSR are acute triangles, which means that angles B and D are both acute angles. But this contradicts equation above, which states that $\angle Q + \angle S = 180$.

② Assume that AC>25.
   Then, triangles ABC and ADC are obtuse triangles, which means that angles B and D are both obtuse angles.
   Again, this contradicts equation $\angle Q + \angle S = 180$.

Thus, we must have AC=25.

From Pythagorean triple, $\triangle$PQR (7-24-25) and $\triangle$PSR (15-20-25) are right triangles.
So, $\angle Q = \angle S = 90$ and
by the Inscribed Angle Theorem, PR is a diameter of the circle.

Now the area of the circle is $\pi \left(\frac{25}{2}\right)^2 = \frac{625}{4}\pi$ and
the area of $\triangle$PQR is $\frac{1}{2} \times 7 \times 24 = 84$ and $\triangle$PSR is $\frac{1}{2} \times 15 \times 20 = 150$.

Therefore, the area between the circle and the quadrilateral is;
$$\frac{625}{4}\pi - 84 - 150 = \frac{625\pi - 936}{4}$$
and $x + y + z = 625 + 936 + 4 = 1565$.

34. **Answer** (B)

From Pythagorean triple (16-30-34), $\triangle WXY$ is a right triangle so, WY is a diameter of the circle. And $\angle Z$ is a right angle by Inscribed Angle Theorem and $\triangle WZY$ is also a triangle. So, $WZ = \sqrt{34^2 - 14^2} = 8\sqrt{5}$.

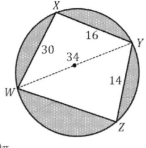

① area of circle

$$\pi\left(\frac{34}{2}\right)^2 = 289\pi$$

② area of quadrilateral $WXYZ$

$$\frac{1}{2} \times 16 \times 30 + \frac{1}{2} \times 14 \times 8\sqrt{5} = 240 + 56\sqrt{15}$$

Therefore, the area between the circle and the quadrilateral is;
$$289\pi - 240 - 56\sqrt{15}$$
and $a + b + c + d = 289 + 240 + 56 + 15 = 600$.

35. **Answer** (D)

We denote by P the circle that has the equation $x^2 + y^2 = 4$, by Q that $x^2 + y^2 = 64$, and by R that $(x - 5)^2 + y^2 = 3$. Also, we denote by C a circle that is tangent to P, Q, and R, and by (a,b) the coordinates of circle C, and r the radius of this circle.

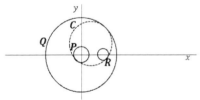

From the graphs of circles P, Q, R, we observe that if C is tangent to all of them, then C must be internally tangent to Q. We have
$a^2 + b^2 = (8 - r)^2$. (1)
We do the following casework analysis in terms of whether C is externally tangent to P and R.
Case 1: C is externally tangent to P and R.
we have $a^2 + b^2 = (r + 2)^2$ (2)
and $(a - 5)^2 + b^2 = \left(r + \sqrt{3}\right)^2$. (3)
Taking (2) − (1), we get $(r + 2)^2 - (8 - r)^2 = 0$. Thus, $r = 3$.

Case 2: P is internally tangent to C, R is externally tangent to C.
we have $a^2 + b^2 = (r - 2)^2$ (4)

and $(a - 5)^2 + b^2 = \left(r + \sqrt{3}\right)^2$.   (5)

Taking $(4) - (1)$, we get $(r - 2)^2 - (8 - r)^2 = 0$. Thus, $r = 5$.

Case 3: P is externally tangent to C, R is internally tangent to C.
we have $a^2 + b^2 = (r + 2)^2$ (6)

and $(a - 5)^2 + b^2 = \left(r - \sqrt{3}\right)^2$.   (7)

Taking $(6) - (1)$, we get $(r + 2)^2 - (8 - r)^2 = 0$. Thus, $r = 3$.

Case 4: P is internally tangent to C, R is internally tangent to C.
we have $a^2 + b^2 = (r - 2)^2$ (8)

and $(a - 5)^2 + b^2 = \left(r - \sqrt{3}\right)^2$.   (9)

Taking $(8) - (1)$, we get $(r - 2)^2 - (8 - r)^2 = 0$. Thus, $r = 5$.

Because the graph is symmetric with the x-axis, and for each case above, the solution of b is not 0. Hence, in each case, there are two congruent circles whose centers are symmetric through the x-axis.

Therefore, the sum of the areas of all the circles in C is
$$2(3^2\pi + 5^2\pi + 3^2\pi + 5^2\pi) = 136\pi.$$

We denote by P the circle that has the equation $x^2 + y^2 = 16$, by Q that $x^2 + y^2 = 36$, and by R that $(x + 6)^2 + y^2 = 5$. Also, we denote by C a circle that is tangent to P, Q, and R, and by (a, b) the coordinates of circle C, and r the radius of this circle.

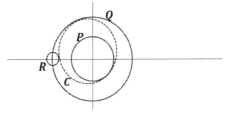

From the graphs of circles P, Q, R, we observe that if C is tangent to all of them, then C must be internally tangent to Q. We have
$a^2 + b^2 = (6 - r)^2$.　　　　(1)
We do the following casework analysis in terms of whether C is externally tangent to P and R.
Case 1: C is externally tangent to P and R.
we have $a^2 + b^2 = (r + 4)^2$　　　(2)
and $(a + 6)^2 + b^2 = \left(r + \sqrt{5}\right)^2$.　　(3)
Taking (2) − (1), we get $(r + 4)^2 - (6 - r)^2 = 0$. Thus, $r = 1$.
Case 2: P is internally tangent to C, R is externally tangent to C.
we have $a^2 + b^2 = (r - 4)^2$　　　(4)
and $(a + 6)^2 + b^2 = \left(r + \sqrt{5}\right)^2$.　　(5)
Taking (4) − (1), we get $(r - 4)^2 - (6 - r)^2 = 0$. Thus, $r = 5$.
Case 3: P is externally tangent to C, R is internally tangent to C.
we have $a^2 + b^2 = (r + 4)^2$　　　　(6)
and $(a + 6)^2 + b^2 = \left(r - \sqrt{5}\right)^2$.　　　(7)
Taking (6) − (1), we get $(r + 4)^2 - (6 - r)^2 = 0$. Thus, $r = 1$.
Case 4: P is internally tangent to C, R is internally tangent to C.
we have $a^2 + b^2 = (r - 4)^2$　　　　(8)
and $(a + 6)^2 + b^2 = \left(r + \sqrt{5}\right)^2$.　　　(9)
Taking (8) − (1), we get $(r - 4)^2 - (6 - r)^2 = 0$. Thus, $r = 1$.

Because the graph is symmetric with the x-axis, and for each case above, the solution of b is not 0. Hence, in each case, there are two congruent circles whose centers are symmetric through the x-axis.
Therefore, the sum of the areas of all the circles in C is
$$2(1^2\pi + 5^2\pi + 1^2\pi + 5^2\pi) = 104\pi.$$

First, extend segments AD and BE until they meet at point G. Since AB is parallel to ED, we have $\angle ABG = \angle DEG$ and $\angle GDE = \angle GAB$, so $\triangle ABG \sim \triangle DEG$ by AA.

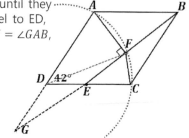

Because $ABCD$ is a rhombus, $AB = CD = 2DE$. Thus, $AG = 2GD$, which means that D is the midpoint of AG.

Now, let's consider $\triangle GFA$. We know that $AF \perp BE$, so $\triangle GFA$ is a right triangle. Also, we know that FD is the median of $\triangle GFA$, which means that $FD = AD$. (D is the midpoint of AG)

Because $ABCD$ is a rhombus, $FD = AD = CD$. Therefore, there exists a circle with center D and radius AD that passes through F, A, and C. This means that $\angle GFC = \angle GAC = \left(\frac{1}{2}\right) \times \angle GDC$. (from Central Angle and Inscribed Angle relation)

Therefore, $\angle GFC = \frac{1}{2} \times \angle GDC = \frac{1}{2} \times (180° - 42°) = 69°$ and $\angle BFC$ is $180 - 69 = 111°$.

38. Answer (D)

Extending PS and QT to point X, as shown below:

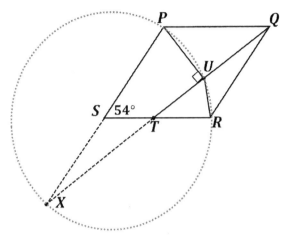

From given, $PQ = SR$ and $ST = TR = \frac{1}{2}SR = \frac{1}{2}PQ$ and $\angle XST = \angle XPQ$, $\angle XTS = \angle XQP$. So, $\triangle XST \backsim \triangle XPQ$ with ratio of $2:1$ and $PX = 2PS$, S is the midpoint of PX. PS, SR, and SX are radius of a circle. For an arc $\overset{\frown}{XR}$, $\angle XSR$ is the central angle and $\angle XUR$ is the inscribed angle.

So,

$\angle XUR = \frac{1}{2}\angle XST = \frac{1}{2}(180 - 54°) = 63°$ and $\angle QUR = 180 - 63 = 117°$.

39. Answer (B)

Let us assume that the index card is a rectangle $ABCD$. Vertex B and vertex D cut out equal squares of side 1cm. Let the coordinates of D be $(0,0)$ and the coordinates of B be (x,y), where x and

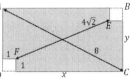

y represent the width and length of the index card, respectively. After cutting out the squares, two new vertices E and F are formed. The coordinates of E are $(x-1, y-1)$, and the coordinates of F are $(1,1)$. From this information, we can set up the following two equations:

① $AC = 8$, which means that diagonal AC of the rectangle is 8cm.
$$x^2 + y^2 = 64$$

② $EF = 4\sqrt{2}$, which means that distance between the two closest vertices of the squares is $4\sqrt{2}$cm by Pythagorean theorem.

$$EF = \sqrt{(x - 1 - 1)^2 + (y - 1 - 1)^2} = 4\sqrt{2}$$
$$(x - 2)^2 + (y - 2)^2 = \left(4\sqrt{2}\right)^2$$

Expanding this equation:

$$x^2 - 4x + 4 + y^2 - 4y + 4 = 32$$
$$x^2 + y^2 - 4x - 4y + 8 = 32$$
$$64 - 4x - 4y + 8 = 32$$
$$4x + 4y = 40 \quad \rightarrow \quad x + y = 10$$

From $x + y = 10$ and $x^2 + y^2 = 64$;

$$(x + y)^2 = 10^2 \quad \rightarrow \quad x^2 + 2xy + y^2 = 100$$

So,

$$64 + 2xy = 100 \quad \rightarrow \quad 2xy = 36 \quad \rightarrow \quad xy = 18$$

Therefore, the area $(x \times y)$ of rectangle is $xy = 18$.

40. **Answer** (**D**)

Let the dimensions of the cardboard be x and y.
Using the Pythagorean theorem;
$$x^2 + y^2 = 10^2 = 100$$
$$(x - 2)^2 + (y - 2)^2 = \left(2\sqrt{13}\right)^2 = 52$$
$$\rightarrow x^2 - 4x + 4 + y^2 - 4y + 4 = 52$$
$$\rightarrow 100 + 8 - 4x - 4y = 52$$
$$\rightarrow -4x - 4y = -56 \quad \rightarrow \quad x + y = 14$$
This means that;
$$(x + y)^2 = 14^2 \quad \rightarrow \quad x^2 + 2xy + y^2 = 196$$
$$100 + 2xy = 196 \quad \rightarrow \quad xy = 48$$

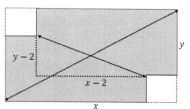

Therefore, the area $(x \times y)$ of rectangle is $xy = 48$.

41. **Answer** **(B)**

We can begin by noticing that the bowl is made up of four regular hexagons, a square and four triangles. Extend line segments a, and b to their point of concurrency.

X and Y are regular hexagons, with interiors composed of 6 equilateral triangles. When one equilateral triangle is expanded from each hexagon, the resulting triangles meet at point P. These two triangles are also equilateral and have a side length of 2.

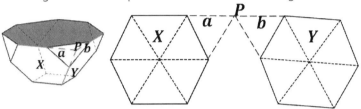

In the top plane of the bowl, octagon has four pairs of parallel sides and the octagon is contained within the square created by extending sides a and b.
So, the area is

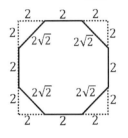

$$6^2 - 4 \times \left(\frac{1}{2} \times 2 \times 2\right) = 28.$$

Therefore, the area of the octagon is 28.

42. **Answer** **(C)**

The lateral faces of the 3D shape consist of three squares and three equilateral triangles.

 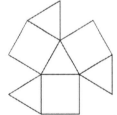 

In the top plane of the bowl, area of a regular hexagon with a side length of 2 is found using 6 equilateral triangles.

$$6 \times \frac{\sqrt{3}}{4} \times 2^2 = 6\sqrt{3}$$

Therefore, the area of the hexagon is $6\sqrt{3}$.

| 43. | **Answer** | (**D**) |

We know that $PS = PX + XS = 6 + 8 = 10$. Also, since PQRS is a rhombus, $PQ = PS = 10$. Triangle PQX is a 6-8-10 right triangle, so $QX = 8$ (using the Pythagorean theorem).

To find the area of the rhombus, we use the formula for the area of a parallelogram: base× height. So, $8 \times 10 = 80$.

| 44. | **Answer** | (**B**) |

$\triangle ABE$ is a 5-12-13 right triangle so, BE=12. Since □ABCD is an isosceles trapezoid, AD=5+15+5=25.

Therefore, the area of □ABCD is:
$$= \frac{1}{2}(15 + 25) \times 12 = 240.$$

| 45. | **Answer** | (**D**) |

Suppose that $\overline{BD}$ intersect $\overline{AP}$ and $\overline{AC}$ at X and Y. $\triangle ABX \cong \triangle AYX$, by ASA congruency.
Let $\overline{AB} = \overline{AY} = 2x$.
By using the Angle Bisector Theorem,
$$\frac{\overline{AB}}{\overline{AC}} = \frac{\overline{BP}}{\overline{CP}} \rightarrow \frac{2x}{\overline{AC}} = \frac{2}{3} \rightarrow \overline{AC} = 3x, \quad \overline{YC} = x$$

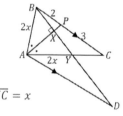

Note that ∠YCB and ∠YAD are congruent since they are alternate interior angles formed. Similarly, ∠YBC and ∠YDA are congruent. Thus, $\triangle CBY$ and $\triangle ADY$ are similar by AA Similarity.
$$\frac{AY}{CY} = \frac{AD}{BC} \rightarrow \frac{2x}{x} = \frac{AD}{5} \rightarrow \overline{AD} = 10$$

Therefore, $\overline{AD}$ is equal to 10.

46. *Answer* **(E)**

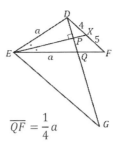

Suppose that $\overline{DG}$ intersect $\overline{EX}$ and $\overline{EF}$ at P and Q. $\triangle EDP \cong \triangle EQP$, by ASA congruency.
Let $\overline{ED} = \overline{EQ} = a$.
By using the Angle Bisector Theorem,

$$\frac{\overline{ED}}{\overline{EF}} = \frac{\overline{DX}}{\overline{FX}} \rightarrow \frac{a}{\overline{EF}} = \frac{4}{5} \rightarrow \overline{EF} = \frac{5}{4}a, \qquad \overline{QF} = \frac{1}{4}a$$

Note that $\angle QFD$ and $\angle QEG$ are congruent since they are alternate interior angles formed. Similarly, $\angle QDF$ and $\angle QGE$ are congruent. Thus, $\triangle FDQ$ and $\triangle EGQ$ are similar by AA Similarity.

$$\frac{EQ}{QF} = \frac{EG}{DF} \rightarrow \frac{a}{\frac{1}{4}a} = \frac{EG}{9} \rightarrow \overline{EG} = 36$$

Therefore, $\overline{EG}$ is equal to 36.

47. *Answer* **(B)**

Label the points on the diagram as shown in the figure below: Using angle chasing, we find that $\triangle ABC \backsim \triangle CDE \backsim \triangle EFG$.
Since $AB = 8$ and $AC = 10$, $\triangle ABC$ is a 6-8-10 right triangle with $BC = 6$. Also, $CE = 10$, $CD = 8$, and $DE = 6$. $EF = DF - DE = 8 - 6 = 2$.

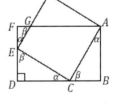

Using the similar triangles, EF is $\frac{2}{8} = \frac{1}{4}$ of the corresponding AB, so FG is $\frac{1}{4} \times 6 = \frac{3}{2}$.

Calculating area of three triangles:

$$\triangle ABC = \frac{1}{2} \times 6 \times 8 = 24, \qquad \triangle CDE = \frac{1}{2} \times 8 \times 6 = 24,$$

$$\triangle EFG = \frac{1}{2} \times 2 \times \frac{3}{2} = \frac{3}{2} \rightarrow 24 + 24 + \frac{3}{2} = \frac{99}{2} = 49.5$$

Therefore, the area of the overlapping is
$$8 \times 14 - 49.5 = 112 - 49.5 = 62.5$$

48. **Answer** (D)

Let a be the area of ADE.

$\triangle PUV \sim \triangle PST$ (by AA) with side length ratio $4:5$.

So, area ratio is $\dfrac{4^2}{5^2} = \dfrac{16}{25}$ and

the area of $\triangle PUV$ is $\dfrac{16}{25}a$.

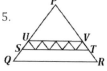

Note that a is comprised of the 9 small isosceles triangles and a triangle $\triangle PUV$.

Thus, we have:

$$a = 9 + \frac{16}{25}a \quad \rightarrow \quad \frac{9}{25}a = 9 \quad \rightarrow \quad a = 25$$

Therefore, the area of trapezoid $QSTR$ is $50 - 25 = 25$.

49. **Answer** (E)

There are two cases for the before transformed configuration:
Case 1) the center square is filled:
Exactly two of the eight adjacent neighboring squares of the center are filled. The only possibility is that the squares along one diagonal are filled.
There are 2 such configurations.

Case 2) the center square is empty
Exactly three of the eight adjacent neighboring squares of the center are filled. We have four possibilities for the before transformed configuration, as shown below:

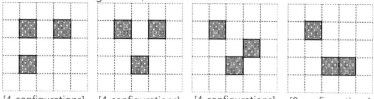

[4 configurations]   [4 configurations]   [4 configurations]   [8 configurations]

In this case, there are $4+4+4+8=20$ possible before transformed configurations.

Therefore, the total number of initial configurations that lead to a transformed grid consisting of a single filled square in the center after a single transformation is $2 + 20 = 22$.

50. **Answer** (**D**)

Visualize the two transformations by drawing:

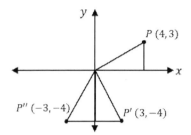

Using distance formula,
$$d = \sqrt{(-3-4)^2 + (-4-3)^2} = 7\sqrt{2}.$$

51. **Answer** **(D)**

To find the pattern of angles at which the point (1,0) ends up after each transformation $R_1, R_2, R_3, \ldots R_n$, we start by considering the initial point $P(1,0)$ at $0°$.

After applying R_1, P is rotated to $1°$ counterclockwise and reflected across the y-axis. So, after applying P1, final position is $179°$.

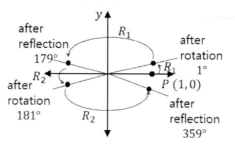

- R_2 brings P to $181°$ (rotation $2°$) and then to $359°$ (reflection)
- R_3 brings P to $2°$ (rotation $3°$) and then to $178°$ (reflection)
- R_4 brings P to $182°$ (rotation $4°$) and then to $358°$ (reflection)
- R_5 brings P to $3°$ (rotation $5°$) and then to $177°$ (reflection)
- R_6 brings P to $183°$ (rotation $6°$) and then to $357°$ (reflection)
...

After each transformation, the angle of the final position is;
$179°(R_1), 359°(R_2), 178°(R_3), 358°(R_4), 177°(R_5), 357°(R_6), \ldots$.
Dividing it into odd and even numbered position;
① odd numbered position
$\qquad$ $179°(R_1),$ $\qquad$ $178°(R_3),$ $\qquad$ $177°(R_5),$ $\qquad$ ...
so, at $(2k-1)$th position
$$R_{2k-1} = (180-k)°$$
② even numbered position
$\qquad$ $359°(R_2),$ $\qquad$ $358°(R_4),$ $\qquad$ $357°(R_6), \ldots$
so, at $(2k)$th position
$$R_{2k} = (360-k)°$$

To return the point (1,0) back to itself, the final angle should be $0°$. Thus, we need to find the value of n that satisfies the equation $180° - k = 0°$ or $360° - k = 0°$

The least such positive integer k is 180.

Therefore, the smallest positive integer value of n is
$$n = 2k - 1 = 2(180) - 1 = 359.$$

To find the pattern of angles at which the point (1,1) ends up after each transformation $T_1, T_2, T_3, \ldots T_n$, we start by considering the initial point $P(1,1)$. The angle of the initial point (1,1) is 45°.

After applying T_1, P is reflected across the x-axis and rotated to 1° counterclockwise. So, after applying P1, final position is −44°.

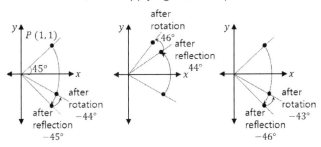

- T_2 brings P to 44° (reflection) and then to 46° (rotation 2°)
- T_3 brings P to −46° (reflection) and then to −43° (rotation 3°)
- T_4 brings P to 43° (reflection) and then to 47° (rotation 4°)
- T_5 brings P to −47° (reflection) and then to −42° (rotation 5°)
- T_6 brings P to 42° (reflection) and then to 48° (rotation 6°)

...

After each transformation, the angle of the final position is;
$-44°(T_1), 46°(T_2), -43°(T_3), 47°(T_4), -42°(T_5), 48°(T_6), \ldots$.
Dividing it into odd and even numbered position;
① odd numbered position
$$-44°(T_1), \qquad -43°(T_3), \qquad -42°(T_5), \qquad \ldots$$
so, at $(2k-1)$th position
$$T_{2k-1} = (-45 + k)°$$
② even numbered position
$$46°(T_2), \qquad 47°(T_4), \qquad 48°(T_6), \ldots$$
so, at $(2k)$th position
$$T_{2k} = (45 + k)°$$

To return the point (1,1) back to itself, the final angle should be 45°. Thus, we need to find the value of n that satisfies the equation
$-45° + k = 45°$ or $45° + k = 405°$

The least such positive integer k is 90.

Therefore, the smallest positive integer value of n is
$$n = 2k - 1 = 2(90) - 1 = 179.$$

Made in United States
Troutdale, OR
09/22/2024

23031686R00055